Basic Math

Doubling and Multiplying

Richard Leffingwell

Heinemann Library
Chicago, Illinois

Customer Service   888–454–2279
Visit our website at www.heinemannlibrary.com

Photo research by Erica Newbery
Designed by Joanna Hinton-Malivoire
Printed in China by South China Printing Company Limited

10 09 08 07 06
10 9 8 7 6 5 4 3 2 1

Library of Congress Cataloging-in-Publication Data
Leffingwell, Richard.
  Doubling and multiplying / Richard Leffingwell.
     p. cm. -- (Basic math)
  Includes index.
  ISBN 1-4034-8157-1 (library binding-hardcover) -- ISBN 1-4034-8162-8 (pbk.)
 1. Multiplication--Juvenile literature. 2. Arithmetic--Juvenile literature. I. Leake,
Diyan. II. Title.
III. Series: Leffingwell, Richard. Basic math.
  QA115.L4485 2006
  513.2'13--dc22
                              2006005920

Acknowledgments
The author and publisher are grateful to the following for permission to reproduce
copyright material: Getty Images (Photodisc Red/Davies & Starr) p. **22**; Harcourt
Education Ltd (www.mmstudios.co.uk) pp. **4–18**, **20**, back cover

Cover photograph reproduced with permission of Getty Images (DK Images/Andy
Crawford)

Contents

What Is Doubling?

What does it look like when you
see double?

You see two of everything.

Doubling Flowers

2 + 2

When you double 2, you add 2 and 2 together.

2 x 4

You put together two groups that are both the same, 4 and 4.

Adding the same numbers together is also called multiplying.

Doubling Marbles

Look what happens when you keep doubling a number.

Start by doubling 1.

$2 \times 1 = 2$

Now double 2.

$$2 \times 2 = 4$$

$$2 \times 4 = 8$$

Now double 4.

Learning doubles will help you learn multiplication.

Can you double 8?

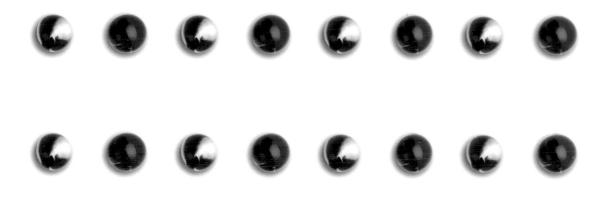

2 x 8 = ?

Doubling Stars

What happens when you double 3?

$$2 \times 3 = ?$$

When you double 3, you add 2 groups of 3 together.

Now try doubling 6.

$$2 \times 6 = ?$$

Can you double 12?

$$2 \times 12 = ?$$

You can keep on doubling as long as you like.

Can you double 24?

It might be hard.

★ ★ ★ ★ ★ ★ ★ ★ ★ ★ ★ ★
★ ★ ★ ★ ★ ★ ★ ★ ★ ★ ★ ★

★ ★ ★ ★ ★ ★ ★ ★ ★ ★ ★ ★
★ ★ ★ ★ ★ ★ ★ ★ ★ ★ ★ ★

$$2 \times 24 = ?$$

Doubling Buttons

What if you double 5?

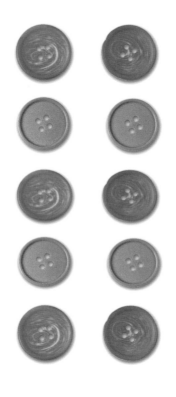

2 x 5 = ?

What if you double 10?

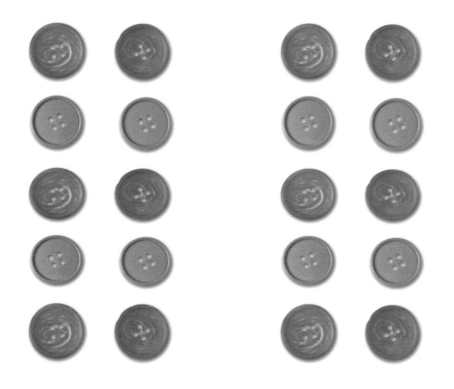

$$2 \times 10 = ?$$

Practicing Doubling

$$2 \times 4 = ?$$

It seems like when you double something you end up with more.

Is this always true?

What would happen if you doubled nothing?

$$2 \times 0 = 0$$

You still have nothing!

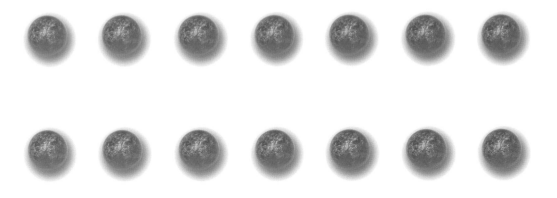

$$2 \times 7 = 14$$

When you double something you are adding the same number.

You are multiplying by 2.

$$2 \times 4 = 8$$

$$2 \times 5 = 10$$

$$2 \times 6 = 12$$

$$2 \times 7 = 14$$

$$2 \times 8 = 16$$

Doubling can be fun.

How old would you be if you doubled your age?

Quiz

Can you answer this doubling question?

$$2 \times 7 = ?$$

Hint: You need to add 2 groups of 7 together.

The "Times" Sign

x   You use this sign to show that you are multiplying numbers.

$$2 \times 3$$

When you multiply 2 by 3, you get 6.

=   You use the equals sign to show what 2 times 3 is equal to.

$$2 \times 3 = 6$$

Index

Answer to the quiz on page 22

$2 \times 7 = 14$

Note to parents and teachers

Reading nonfiction texts for information is an important part of a child's literacy development. Readers can be encouraged to ask simple questions and then use the text to find the answers. Most chapters in this book begin with a question. Read the questions together. Look at the pictures. Talk about what the answer might be. Then read the text to find out if your predictions were correct. To develop readers' enquiry skills, encourage them to think of other questions they might ask about the topic. Discuss where you could find the answers. Assist children in using the contents page, picture glossary, and index to practice research skills and new vocabulary.